I0759638

Štěpánka Sekaninová
Linh Dao

HOW TO BECOME A BUTTERFLY

albatros

MIRACLE ON THE MEADOW

At the very edge of a blooming meadow a miracle is happening! From tiny eggs stuck to the jagged leaves of burning nettles, little caterpillars are hatching. They immediately start eating. Nettles are so tasty! Yum! What's that? Do you hear a whispering sound?

NOT ENOUGH NETTLES

Hi! Here I am! You can call me Amanda. I can't introduce you to my brothers and sisters because there are so many that I don't know all of their names. Our nettle patch is too small for all of us to keep eating, but I'm so hungry my tummy is rumbling non-stop! So I'm going out into the big, wide world to find nettles. I wish I didn't have to leave my brothers and sisters behind, but I want to eat, so what else can I do?

Nettle leaves, nettle leaves, always nettle leaves!
Crunch, crunch...
I'm Victor. Hello there!
Call me Clara.
Hey, almost all the leaves are gone!
I'm Thaddaeus.

SO MANY BUTTERFLIES!

I found a fresh nettle branch with a great view of the meadow. Look at all the colorful butterflies! I've heard that there are 180,000 different species of moths in the world. Out of those, about 18,000 are daytime butterflies like I'm going to be. I look so different from those fancy fliers now, but someday I will have the gorgeous wings, and I'll be able to fly! I must keep eating! *Crunch . . . slurp . . . munch . . .* to grow and grow!

COMMON BRIMSTONE

I'm the yellowest of all yellows, and one of the hardiest butterflies. At winter's end, when new warmth arrives, I fly out of my hiding place. It doesn't matter to me that there is still snow on the ground.

RED ADMIRAL

I'm a born traveler. I fly off in search of sun in winter and return in spring. In summer, I suck nectar from flowers. In autumn, I fortify myself with the juice of rotting fruit. Then I head off to the other side of the world.

SWALLOWTAIL

When faced with an enemy, I give off a smell of fennel, and he flies right out of my way. Pretty effective, eh?

ADONIS BLUE

The most beautiful color in the world is blue. The front of my butterfly array is also sky blue. But when I close my wings, ha, no one would recognize me as a blue butterfly! How about that?

IT'S NOT ALL ABOUT BUTTERFLIES . . .

The more I eat, the more I grow—and the hungrier I get. My tummy is rumbling again. *Munch, munch . . .* and on I go. As I move through the country, I meet lots of different creatures. Some have super-long legs, others stiff elytra to protect their wings. What if I turn not into a butterfly but a little round bug? Look how many of those there are, of all different types!

CRICKET

We crickets are musical virtuosi. No one can perform a more thrilling serenade. Do you know where our hearing organs are? You don't? In our knees!

BEE

I'm aching all over! All day I've been gathering nectar so that my hive will have lots of honey.

BUMBLEBEE

Buzz-zz. I fly around the countryside, pollinating flowers that other bees can't reach. My tongue is really, really long.

SEVEN-SPOTTED LADYBUG

I'm busy rescuing flowers right now, by catching aphids that feed on the leaves. I'm pretty useful.

DUNG BEETLE

My wife and I will make a burrow in this ball of dung. Look, Mary! I've found us a nice home.

NOT EVERYONE IS A FRIEND

Shoosh! Quiet, please! I'm hiding, so don't give me away. There are scary creatures in the meadow who would like nothing more than to sink their teeth into my soft caterpillar body. Before moving off slowly to the nearest nettle, I'll wait for my enemies to lose interest. Wish me well!

WASP

Buzz-zz. What can I catch for my hungry larvae waiting at home? A chubby caterpillar would be ideal.

WART-BITER

Hop, jump, hop, jump. My strong legs need lots of nutrients. Hop, jump. What will I catch?

BIRDS

Cheep, cheep, peck.
Caterpillars? Worms?
Where are you hiding?

SPIDERS

I'm weaving my web.
Who shall I catch in
it? Which meat will
I ensnare for lunch?

CATERPILLAR-HUNTER BEETLE

If you value your life,
get out of my way.
Chubby larvae are my
very favorite snack.

Are there
any caterpillars
about?

ANT ARMY

Left, right, left, right, halt!
Caterpillar located.
Prepare the attack!

WE CAN DEFEND OURSELVES

Don't worry! We caterpillars aren't completely helpless. We defend ourselves bravely and effectively, each in our own way, by making life poisonous or otherwise unpleasant for those who hunt us.

GO AWAY! YUCK!

When a lone caterpillar of the cabbage butterfly encounters an enemy, guess what it does? It dumps all its stomach juices and undigested food on the foe! Yuck! This makes that caterpillar less than appetizing.

WATCH OUT! POISON!

Caterpillars of the magnificent American monarch butterfly are poisonous because parents lay eggs on poisonous plant leaves, which their caterpillars will feast on. Not only is this food all theirs, but no predator will want to eat their poisonous bodies.

BRITTLE HAIRS

A red admiral caterpillar is covered with dense, prickly hair connected to the venom glands. The points of the hair prick attackers, before breaking off and releasing poison into the wound—so saving the caterpillar.

BLENDING IN

Some of us who are neither poisonous nor hairy can make ourselves invisible. We blend in with our surroundings so that not even the keenest-eyed observer will spot us.

CATERPILLAR OR SNAKE?

Hiss-ss-ss . . . there's a dangerous, venomous snake crawling around. Run for your lives! Looking like a snake is a highly effective method of defense.

Hiss-ss-ss . . .

I'M HUNGRY!!!

I know that I keep repeating myself, but my main task is to eat and grow. Since the beginning of this book, I have grown much bigger and stronger! When I emerged from my egg, I was tiny and skinny. Now I'm a big, sturdy caterpillar who feels in her nonexistent bones that she's about to pupate.

Zzz

A LITTLE REST BEFORE THE ACTION

Before I shed my skin, I need a little rest. I'll stop eating and simply lie here and wait for what's to come. You might want to go out and play, or read a book, because my waiting may take several days. See you later, then!

ABOUT TO MOLT

When *you* grow, your skin grows with you. This doesn't happen with caterpillars. To grow, we need to take off our old skin, which is getting tight. Today, my skin feels tight everywhere. I must be about to shed my skin—or molt.

IN THREE DAYS

See? The old skin has become see-through like a veil around my body. It is time for me to change my coat.

SELF-INFLATION

While you change your T-shirts effortlessly, our undressing is difficult. We have to significantly increase our volume. And so we try to expand and grow with all our might.

I JUST GOT BIGGER

Look how huge I am, almost like a balloon. *Zip!* Now the skin behind my head bursts open, and I slowly twist and inflate to slip out of my old skin.

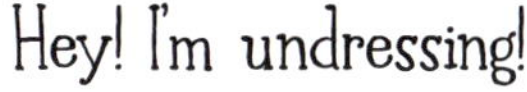

AND IT FEELS GREAT...

Being in my new coat is a wonderful feeling. My body can stretch in all directions. *Yee-ee, aah-aah...* That's it! I'm hungry. Please excuse me—I'm off to eat the most nettles the world has ever seen.

HOW DO I LOOK?

Take a good look at me, because I'm about to pupate. How long does the caterpillar period last? I can't give you a precise answer: it depends on its food. The change comes more quickly for a caterpillar that eats well than for one that doesn't.

I'M A HEAD AND 13 SEGMENTS

Look at my thorax and you will see three pairs of prolegs with little claws on the end. These help me hold my food without dropping it, allowing me to eat in peace.

LEGS AND PROLEGS

I have legs and prolegs, each with a hook on the end. These allow me to cling to any surface that isn't as smooth as glass.

THE EYES HAVE IT

My head has six pairs of eyes! It also has mouthparts with powerful mandibles that allow me to eat my fill. I even have short antennae and dangerous spines on my body!

Don't you think that I've grown enormous?

Ugh! Crawling is a struggle. I'm ready for my great change.

I'M PUPATING

I'm about to stop being fun to be with, so let me apologize in advance. Right now, my main interest is in finding a place where I can pupate and come of age in peace and safety. I'm so looking forward to spreading my butterfly wings and flying over the meadow for the first time! Am I sure that I'll become a butterfly? Yes, I am. Now to find that hiding place!

This pupation is no joke! You have to spin a little bundle of threads on a plant twig. So please, let me get to work now.

ENGAGED?!

All the gaps, holes, and places under stones are already occupied. I've been too slow! What am I to do? I'll just have to pupate on a plant.

Now I'm attaching myself to the fiber and dropping my head. After this I'll just wait.

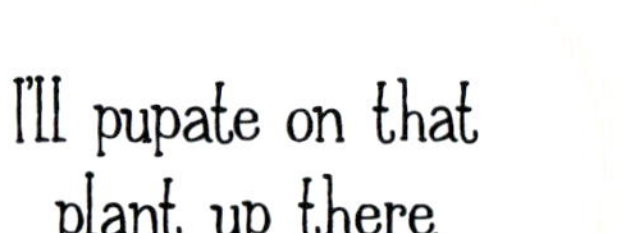

1
3
This waiting is pretty boring, I must say. I'm wriggling about to pass the time.
2
4
Oh, I'm almost done! The skin behind my neck has cracked. I'm molting one last time!
5
I'm a chrysalis. Hurray!

METAMORPHOSIS

Amanda the caterpillar—sorry, chrysalis—is entering the last stage. She is about to emerge from her cocoon and come into the world as a butterfly! I wonder what she will look like. If you would like to know, take a look at this miracle with me.

STEP 1

The head end of the pupa splits open.

STEP 2

Peek-a-boo! I'm here . . . and I'm a butterfly!

STEP 3

The butterfly slides out, ever so slowly. Hi! Do you recognize me? I'm Amanda! All wrinkled and wet. I need to hang for an hour or two to dry off.

STEP 4

And now I'm a butterfly. But my wings are still crumpled. Before I can raise and stretch them I must hang with my wings down and wait for hemolymph—similar to your blood—to flow into them. It won't be long now, I can tell!

Look at me! I'm flying! I'm a peacock butterfly with beautiful eye spots to scare away predators. Now I understand! The nettles! Nettles are a peacock butterfly's main food. I'm flying! See you on the next page!

I CAN FLY

Flying over the countryside is wonderful. So much better than trudging through the world as a caterpillar, seeing everything only from the ground. Still, I have to admit—my caterpillar childhood had its own kind of magic. I wonder how my brothers and sisters are doing. Maybe I'll run into them in a meadow sometime soon.

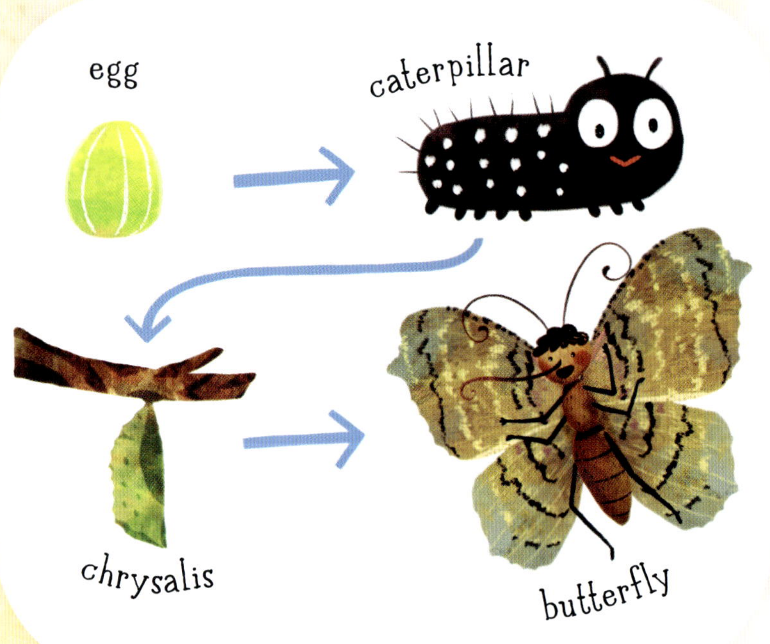

LOOKING BACK . . .

I started out as an egg. After that I was a caterpillar, and then a chrysalis, and now I'm a butterfly! This process of development is known as *metamorphosis*.

1. BUTTERFLY WINGS

My two pairs of wings are covered with tiny, overlapping scales that cause them to change colors beautifully.

2. A BUTTERFLY'S MOUTH

Do you see that long proboscis? This straw-like mouthpart is how I suck nectar. Usually, the proboscis is curled away. But as soon as our feet sense something delicious, it hungrily reaches for a taste.

3. ANTENNAE

As well as making a charming crown for a butterfly's head, antennae allow us to enjoy nature's many scents.

4. A BUTTERFLY'S BODY

Our bodies consist of a head, thorax, and abdomen, and we are covered all over with fine hair.

5. BUTTERFLY LEGS

Long legs for walking, with hairy soles, grow out of the thorax. Believe it or not, we butterflies taste through the soles of our feet!

BUTTERFLIES AT NIGHT?

I'm quite worn out from flying around all day. The sun is setting, and I am waiting for the night. Butterflies don't sleep as humans do. At dusk, we crawl into a cosy crevice, where we rest and get our strength back. I'm talking about diurnal butterflies here, of course. Nocturnal butterflies, usually called moths, fly out at night. Have a look at them while I—yawn, yawn—take a little break.

SWARMS OF NOCTURNAL MOTHS

A moonlit night is a paradise for many moths. Once out and about in the world, they settle on various plants, and not just the nicest, most colorful ones. They care little for a plant's appearance, they are attracted by its scent. This is important, because they pollinate flowers not reached in daytime.

DIURNAL BUTTERFLIES

Diurnal butterflies are never seen at night. If a nocturnal moth is disturbed during the day, it will still fly. There are even some moths that are active in the daytime.

TIME TO SLEEP

Being a butterfly is amazing, and well worth the trouble of metamorphosis and dodging the dangers of sharp bird beaks. Now the sun's heat is getting ever weaker. The leaves are turning golden; winter is approaching. I'm preparing to sleep. And I'm not alone: there are other peacock butterflies with me. We've found a place to sleep in an abandoned cellar. So, good night to you! See you again in spring.

Zzz, zzz,
zzzz…

FINDING A PARTNER

After the long winter, I feel stiff. I need to warm up in the sun and build my strength for an important mission. Before I can lay a clutch of eggs destined to become butterflies, I must find a partner. Now that my strength is back, I spread my wings and fly. The world is beautiful and filled with opportunity.

MAKING MY CHOICE

How many future suitors have swarmed out this spring! They sit by the path, wings outspread to show off their colorful eyespots. Dazzling beauty is what butterflies are all about. I have made my choice. The one on the end has a lovely smile, don't you think?

A BUTTERFLY'S VOICE

Did you know that butterflies make sounds? I rub my wings to make a hiss or a clicking sound to startle predators. This sound is so quiet that humans hardly ever hear it. Right now, my intended is clicking at other butterfly males, to drive them away from me.

COURTSHIP

A butterfly courtship goes like this. The males show off their wings to us females. Each of us chooses her favorite. Then she displays her own beauty in return. I'm so glad that my suitor likes me.

A NEW GENERATION

I'm so happy—because I'm going to be a mom! I've laid a lot of eggs. Newborn butterflies look like peas in a pod to their parents. What shall we name ours? One will be Amanda (after me) and another will be Francis (after his dad), for sure. We could also have a Riley, a Noah, a Liam, an Isabella . . . Can you help me out with the names?

There's so much going on! See the other female laying her eggs? Let's not disturb her as she performs her important task. Elsewhere, a new caterpillar is entering the world. What kind of butterfly will it grow into, I wonder....
Goodbye! Be kind to us butterflies!

HOW TO BECOME A BUTTERFLY

5. května 1746/22, Prague 4, Czech Republic
Author: Štěpánka Sekaninová
Illustrator: © Linh Dao, 2024
Editor: Susan Marston
Translator: Andrew Oakland
Proofreader: Susan Marston
Graphics and typesetting: Adéla Imreczeová,
Kristýna Krahulcová, Roman Havlice

Printed in China by Leo Paper Products Ltd.

www.albatrosbooks.com

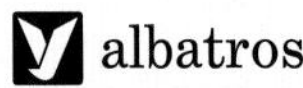